Knitted Leaves

Mini Leaf Scarf Collection to Knit
Designed by Grace Mcewen

This collection is dedicated to all the individuals who think a home made gift is slightly more lovely than the best bought gift.

Happy Knitting!!

Contents

Dahlia Scarf	1
Lacy Vine Scarf	3
Fern	6
Garden Wave	9
Oats Scarf	11

Dahlia Scarf

Grace Mcewen Knitting Pattern Designs

Materials Needed:

Size 7(4.5 mm) straight knitting needles

1 ball of Martha Stewart Extra Soft Wool Blend 65% acrylic, 35% wool 165 yards

Darning Needle

Abbreviations:

K—knit

Ssk—slip one stitch as if to knit, Slip another stitch as if to knit. Insert left-hand needle into front of these 2 stitches and knit them together

K2tog—Knit two stitches together as one stitch

Yo—Yarn over

(kpk) in 1—knit, purl and knit again all in the same st to make 3 sts from 1

dbl dec—Slip first and second stitches together as if to knit. Knit 1 stitch. Pass two slipped stitches over the knit stitch.

Make 1 (m1) - Make one by lifting strand in between stitch just worked and the next stitch, knit into back of this thread.

Pattern Notes:

Dahlia is a fun and fairly easy lace scarf that can be knit long or short depending on the knitter's preference. Any yarn will do to make a lovely scarf , just change the needles to the size recommended by the yarn company on the new yarn.

If you enjoy knitting lace you will enjoy knitting this fast moving scarf.

Dahlia Scarf

Co 21 stitches on size 7(4.5 mm) straight knitting needles

All even rows are worked as purls. The yarn overs are purled.. Once you have repeated the pattern to the desired length complete to row 19 and then bind off on wrong side   The sample is knitted with a repeat of 5 times each side and then bound off. The scarf is knit in two pieces and sewn together on the cast on edge. If desired a provisional cast on may be used.

R1 (RS): k4, k2tog, k4, yo, m1, yo, (kpk) in 1, yo, m1, yo, k4, ssk, k4 (27 stitches)

R3: k3, k2tog, k4, yo, k2, yo, k2tog, yo, (kpk) in 1, yo, ssk, yo, k2, yo, k4, ssk, k3 (31 stitches)

R5: k2, k2tog, k4, yo, k3, yo, k2tog, yo, k2tog, yo, k1, yo, ssk, yo, ssk, yo, k3, yo, k4, ssk, k2 (33 stitches)

R7: k1, k2tog, k4, yo, k4, yo, k2tog, yo, k2tog, yo, dbl dec, yo, ssk, yo, ssk, yo, k4, yo, k4, ssk, k1 (33 stitches)

R9: k2tog, k4, yo, k4, ssk, yo, ssk, yo, ssk, yo, k1, yo, k2tog, yo, k2tog, yo, k2tog, k4, yo, k4, ssk (33 stitches)

R11: k4, k2tog, k4, yo, ssk, yo, ssk, yo, ssk, k1, k2tog, yo, k2tog, yo, k2tog, yo, k4, ssk, k4 (31 stitches)

R13: k3, k2tog, k4, yo, k1, ssk, yo, ssk, yo, dbl dec, yo, k2tog, yo, k2tog, k1, yo, k4, ssk, k3 (29 stitches)

R15: k2, k2tog, k4, yo, k2, ssk, yo, ssk, k1, k2tog, yo, k2tog, k2, yo, k4, ssk, k2 (27 stitches)

R17: k1, k2tog, k4, yo, k3, ssk, dbl dec, k2tog, k3, yo, k4, ssk, k1 (23 stitches)

R19: k2tog, k4, yo, k4, dbl dec, k4, yo, k4, ssk (21 stitches)

Legend:

☐ knit
Knit stitch

╱ k2tog
Knit two stitches together as one stitch

○ yo
Yarn Over

▨ No Stitch
Placeholder - No stitch made.

M make one
Make one by lifting strand in between stitch just worked and the next stitch, knit into back of this thread.

V (k1 p1 k1) in 1 st
Knit, purl and knit again all in the same st to make 3 sts from 1

╲ ssk
Slip one stitch as if to knit, Slip another stitch as if to knit. Insert left-hand needle into front of these 2 stitches and knit them together

▲ Central Double Dec
Slip first and second stitches together as if to knit. Knit 1 stitch. Pass two slipped stitches over the knit stitch.

Finishing -

Weave all ends

Block as needed

Finished measurements—8 inches by 36 inches . Your choice of yarn and needles may alter measurements

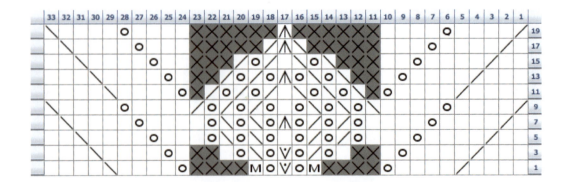

This pattern is strictly for personal use only and cannot be used for commercial or profit without the permission of the designer.

Lacy Vine Scarf

Grace Mcewen Knitting Pattern Designs

Materials Needed:

Size 8(5.0 mm) straight knitting needles

2 balls of Stitch Nation by Debbie Stoller Full O' Sheep 100% Peruvian wool 155 yards

Darning Needle

Cable Needle/Hook

Abbreviations:

K—knit

P—purl

Ssk—slip one stitch as if to knit, Slip another stitch as if to knit. Insert left-hand needle into front of these 2 stitches and knit them together

K2tog—Knit two stitches together as one stitch

P2tog—purl two stitches together as one stitch

K3tog—knit three stitches together as one stitch

P3tog—purl three stitches together as one stitch

Yo—Yarn over

dbl dec—Slip first and second stitches together as if to knit. Knit 1 stitch. Pass two slipped stitches over the knit stitch.

Make 1 (m1) - Make one by lifting strand in between stitch just worked and the next stitch, knit into back of this thread.

Drop1—(D) drop 1 stitch and pull to end of piece. This may require you to pull along depending on the fiber used.

CN—Cable Needle/Hook

c3 over 3 left—sl3 to CN, hold in front. k3, k3 from CN

Pattern Notes:

Lacy Vine is a fast moving, fun scarf to knit. Dainty leaf lace accented with a center cable and drop stitch details adds a Victorian feel to the scarf.

Any yarn will do to make a lovely scarf, just change the needles to the size recommended by the yarn company on the new yarn. When working scarves with drop stitches it is best to use a lofty fiber like wool, hemp or linen.

Lacy Vine Scarf

Co 44 stitches on size 8(5.0 mm) straight knitting needles

The sample is knitted repeating the lace pattern 6 times each side row 1 through row 12 then proceed with Lace Pattern/Chart 2. The scarf is knit in two pieces and sewn together on the cast on edge. If desired a provisional cast on may be used. The stitch count remains consistent at 44 stitches until Lace pattern chart 2 is worked. Please do not slip the first stitch as the pattern will not work properly.

R1 (WS): k3, p14, k2, p6, k2, p14, k3	R7: k3, p14, k2, p6, k2, p14, k3
R2 (RS): p3, k10, k3tog, yo, k1, yo, p2, k6, p2, yo, k1, yo, dbl dec, k10, p3	R8: p3, k4, k3tog, k3, yo, k1, yo, k3, p2, k6, p2, k3, yo, k1, yo, k3, dbl dec, k4, p3
R3: k3, p14, k2, p6, k2, p14, k3	R9: k3, p14, k2, p6, k2, p14, k3
R4: p3, k8, k3tog, k1, yo, k1, yo, k1, p2, k6, p2, k1, yo, k1, yo, k1, dbl dec, k8, p3	R10: p3, k2, k3tog, k4, yo, k1, yo, k4, p2, k6, p2, k4, yo, k1, yo, k4, dbl dec, k2, p3
R5: k3, p14, k2, p6, k2, p14, k3	R11: k3, p14, k2, p6, k2, p14, k3
R6: p3, k6, k3tog, k2, yo, k1, yo, k2, p2, c3 over 3 left, p2, k2, yo, k1, yo, k2, dbl dec, k6, p3	R12: p3, k3tog, k5, yo, k1, yo, k5, p2, c3 over 3 left, p2, k5, yo, k1, yo, k5, dbl dec, p3

Symbol	Description	Symbol	Description
✗	**No Stitch** — Placeholder - No stitch made.	↓	**Drop Stitch** — Drop Stitch
●	**purl** — RS: purl stitch; WS: knit stitch	╲	**ssk** — RS: Slip one stitch as if to knit, Slip another stitch as if to knit. Insert left-hand needle into front of these 2 stitches and knit them together. WS: Purl two stitches together in back loops, inserting needle from the left, behind and into the backs of the 2nd & 1st stitches in that order
□	**knit** — RS: knit stitch; WS: purl stitch		
╱	**k3tog** — RS: Knit three stitches together as one; WS: Purl three stitches together as one	M	**make one** — Make one by lifting strand in between stitch just worked and the next stitch, knit into back of this thread.
O	**yo** — Yarn Over	╱	**k2tog** — Knit two stitches together as one stitch
▲	**Central Double Dec** — Slip first and second stitches together as if to knit. Knit 1 stitch. Pass two slipped stitches over the knit stitch.	╱	**p2tog** — Purl 2 stitches together
⋈⋈	**c3 over 3 left** — sl3 to CN, hold in front, k3, k3 from CN		

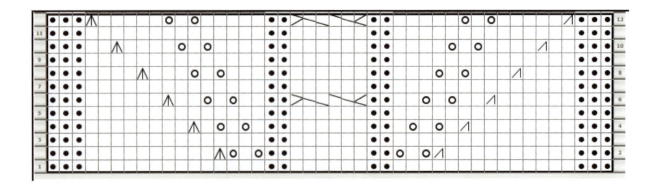

This pattern is strictly for personal use only and cannot be used for commercial or profit without the permission of the designer.

Lacy Vine Scarf

Page 5

Lace Pattern Chart 2

R13: k3, p14, k2, p1, drop1, p2, drop1, p1, k2, p14, k3 (42 Stitches)

R14: p3, k11, k3tog, p2, yo, k1, yo, k2, yo, k1, yo, p2, dbl dec, k11, p3 (42 Stitches)

R15: k3, p12, k2, p8, k2, p12, k3 (42 Stitches)

R16: p3, k9, k3tog, p2, k1, yo, k1, yo, k1, yo, ssk, yo, k1, yo, k1, yo, k1, p2, dbl dec, k9, p3 (43 Stitches)

R17: k3, p10, k2, p13, k2, p10, k3 (43 Stitches)

R18: p3, k7, k3tog, p2, k2, yo, k1, yo, k2, m1, k1, yo, k1, yo, k1, m1, k2, yo, k1, yo, k2, p2, dbl dec, k7, p3 (47 Stitches)

R19: k3, p8, k2, p21, k2, p8, k3 (47 Stitches)

R20: p3, dbl dec, k5, p2, ssk, k5, p1, k2, yo, k1, yo, k2, p1, k5, k2tog, p2, k5, k3tog, p3 (43 stitches)

R21: k3, p6, k2, p6, k1, p7, k1, p6, k2, p6, k3 (43 Stitches)

R22: p3, dbl dec, k3, p2, ssk, k4, p1, k7, p1, k4, k2tog, p2, k3, k3tog, p3 (37 Stitches)

R23: k3, p4, k2, p5, k1, p7, k1, p5, k2, p4, k3 (37 stitches)

R24: p3, ssk, k2tog, p2, ssk, k3, p1, k2, dbl dec, k2, p1, k3, k2tog, p2, ssk, k2tog, p3 (29 stitches)

R25: k3, p2, k2, p4, k1, p5, k1, p4, k2, p2, k3 (29 stitches)

R26: p3, ssk, p2, ssk, k2tog, p1, k1, dbl dec, k1, p1, ssk, k2tog, p2, k2tog, p3 (21 stitches)

R27: k3, p1, k2, p2, k1, p3, k1, p2, k2, p1, k3 (21 stitches)

R28: p3, k1, p2, ssk, p1, dbl dec, p1, k2tog, p2, k1, p3 (17 stitches)

R29: k2, D1, p1, k1, D1, p1, D1, p1, D1, p1, D1, k1, p1, D1, k2 (11 stitches)

R30: p2tog 2 times, k3, p2tog 2 times (7 stitches)

R31: k2tog, p3tog, k2tog (3 Stitches)

R32: dbl dec (1 Stitch)

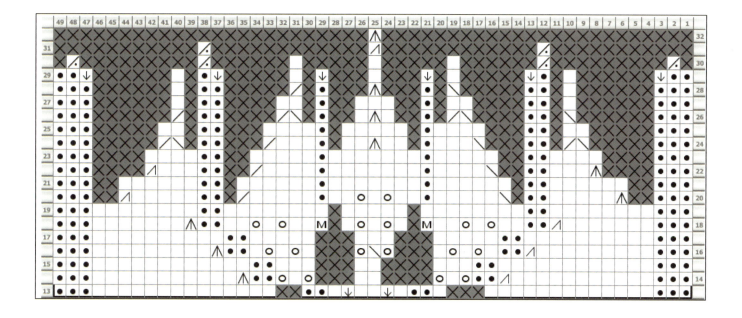

Finishing: Weave all ends , Block as needed

Finished measurements—12 inches by 36 inches . Your choice of yarn and needles may alter measurements

This pattern is strictly for personal use only and cannot be used for commercial or profit without the permission of the designer.

Fern Scarf

Grace Mcewen Knitting Pattern Designs

Abbreviations:

K—knit

P—purl

Ssk—slip one stitch as if to knit, Slip another stitch as if to knit. Insert left-hand needle into front of these 2 stitches and knit them together

K2tog—Knit two stitches together as one stitch

Make one—M -Make one by lifting strand in between stitch just worked and the next stitch, knit into back of this thread.

Dbl dec -Slip first and second stitches together as if to knit. Knit 1 stitch. Pass two slipped stitches over the knit stitch.

DS—Drop Stitch from left hand needle

Materials Needed:

Size 6(4.0 mm) straight knitting needles

1 ball of Knit Picks Gloss Lace Weight Yarn 100% wool 480 yards.

Darning Needle

Pattern Notes:

Fern is a simple to knit, leafy scarf. The scarves leaves are created with a series of drop stitches which adds a light and airy look.

The scarf may be knit with any type of yarn but, will work best with wool, hemp or linen because of the drop stitch..

Fern Scarf

Page 7

Co 71 stitches on size 6 (4.0mm) straight knitting needles

Work 1 row knit and then begin working lace pattern starting on the wrong side.

R1 (WS): (k3, p1, k3, p9, k3, p1, k3, p1,) twice, k3, p1, k3, p9, k3, p1, k3

R2 (RS): (p3, k1, p3, k9, p3, k1, p3, m1, k1, m1), twice, p3, k1, p3, k9, p3, k1, p3

R3: (k3, p1, k3, p9, k3, p1, k3, p3,) twice, k3, p1, k3, p9, k3, p1, k3

R4: (p3, k1, p3, k1, DS, k5, DS, k1, p3, k1, p3, k1, m1, k1, m1, k1,) twice, p3, k1, p3, k1, DS, k5, DS, k1, p3, k1, p3

R5: (k3, p1, k3, p7, k3, p1, k3, p5,) twice, k3, p1, k3, p7, k3, p1, k3

R6: (p3, k1, p3, k2, DS, k1, DS, k2, p3, k1, p3, k2, m1, k1, m1, k2,) twice, p3, k1, p3, k2, DS, k1, DS, k2, p3, k1, p3

R7: (k3, p1, k3, p5, k3, p1, k3, p7,) twice, k3, p1, k3, p5, k3, p1, k3

R8: (p3, k1, p3, ssk, k1, k2tog, p3, k1, p3, k3, m1, k1, m1, k3,) twice, p3, k1, p3, ssk, k1, k2tog, p3, k1, p3

R9: (k3, p1, k3, p3, k3, p1, k3, p9,)twice , k3, p1, k3, p3, k3, p1, k3

R10: (p3, k1, p3, dbl dec, p3, k1, p3, k9,) twice, p3, k1, p3, dbl dec, p3, k1, p3

R11: (k3, p1, k3, p1, k3, p1, k3, p9,) twice, k3, p1, k3, p1, k3, p1, k3

R12: (p3, k1, p3, m1, k1, m1, p3, k1, p3, k1, DS, k5, DS, k1,) twice, p3, k1, p3, m1, k1, m1, p3, k1, p3

R13: (k3, p1, k3, p3, k3, p1, k3, p7), twice, k3, p1, k3, p3, k3, p1, k3

R14: (p3, k1, p3, k1, m1, k1, m1, k1, p3, k1, p3, k2, DS, k1, DS, k2,) twice, p3, k1, p3, k1, m1, k1, m1, k1, p3, k1, p3

R15: (k3, p1, k3, p5,)4 times, k3, p1, k3

R16: (p3, k1, p3, k2, m1, k1, m1, k2, p3, k1, p3, ssk, k1, k2tog), twice, p3, k1, p3, k2, m1, k1, m1, k2, p3, k1, p3

R17: (k3, p1, k3, p7, k3, p1, k3, p3), twice, k3, p1, k3, p7, k3, p1, k3

R18: (p3, k1, p3, k3, m1, k1, m1, k3, p3, k1, p3, dbl dec,) twice, p3, k1, p3, k3, m1, k1, m1, k3, p3, k1, p3

Repeat the pattern from rows 1—18 until garment reaches desired length binding off once row 14 has been completed.

Finishing—Weave all ends and Block as needed

This pattern is strictly for personal use only and cannot be used for commercial or profit without the permission of the designer.

Fern Scarf

Drop Stitch
RS: Drop Stitch

ssk
RS: Slip one stitch as if to knit, Slip another stitch as if to knit. Insert left-hand needle into front of these 2 stitches and knit them together

k2tog
RS: Knit two stitches together as one stitch

Central Double Dec
RS: Slip first and second stitches together as if to knit. Knit 1 stitch. Pass two slipped stitches over the knit stitch.

purl
RS: purl stitch
WS: knit stitch

knit
RS: knit stitch
WS: purl stitch

No Stitch
RS: Placeholder - No stitch made.

make one
RS: Make one by lifting strand in between stitch just worked and the next stitch, knit into back of this thread.

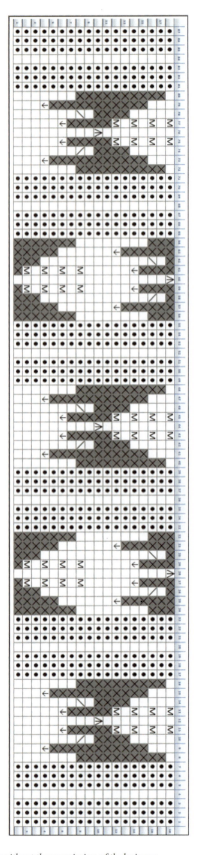

This pattern is strictly for personal use only and cannot be used for commercial or profit without the permission of th designer.

Garden Wave Scarf

Grace Mcewen Knitting Pattern Designs

Page 9

Materials Needed:

Size 7(4.5 mm) straight knitting needles

2 balls of Classic Elite Yarn Firefly 75% viscose, 25% linen, 155 yards.

Darning Needle

Abbreviations:

K—knit

Ssk—lip one stitch as if to knit, Slip another stitch as if to knit. Insert left-hand needle into front of these 2 stitches and knit them together

K2tog—Knit two stitches together as one stitch

Yo—Yarn over

Pattern Notes:

Garden Wave Scarf is an easy way to create a beautiful without mastering complicated stitch . The scarf is all knit with a decrease and increase stitch which creates a delightful wavy look.

Knit with approx 300 yards of yarn this is a fun and easy all year round scarf pattern that can be knit in any type of yarn.

Garden Wave Scarf

Co 40 stitches on size 7(4.5 mm) straight knitting needles

Work 6 rows of all knit. Knitting both right and wrong sides then begin pattern. All even rows are worked in even knit, knitting the yarn overs as well. Once you have repeated the pattern to the desired length complete to row 23 and then work 6 rows in all knit again and then bind off.

R1 (RS <): k4, *ssk, k5, yo, * Repeat from * to * k1
R3: k4, *ssk, k4, yo, k1 * Repeat from * to * k1
R5: k4, *ssk, k3, yo, k2 * Repeat from * to * k1
R7: k4, *ssk, k2, yo, k3 * Repeat from * to * k1
R9: k4, *ssk, k1, yo, k4 * Repeat from * to * k1
R11: k4, *ssk, yo, k5 * Repeat from * to * k1
R13: k1, * yo, k5, k2tog, * Repeat from * to * k4
R15: k1 * k1, yo, k4, k2tog, * Repeat from * to * k4
R17: k1 * k2, yo, k3, k2tog, * Repeat from * to * k4
R19: k1, * k3 yo, k2, k2tog, * Repeat from * to * k4
R21: k1 * k4, yo, k1, k2tog, * Repeat from * to * k4

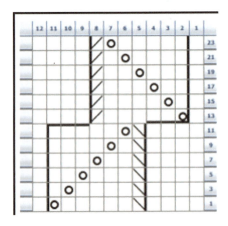

Finishing -

Weave all ends

Block as needed

☐	**knit** — knit stitch
╲	**ssk** — Slip one stitch as if to knit, Slip another stitch as if to knit. Insert left-hand needle into front of these 2 stitches and knit them together
○	**yo** — Yarn Over
╱	**k2tog** — Knit two stitches together as one stitch

This pattern is strictly for personal use only and cannot be used for commercial or profit without the permission of the designer.

Oats Scarf

Grace Mcewen Knitting Pattern Designs

Abbreviations:

K—knit

P—purl

Ssk—slip one stitch as if to knit, Slip another stitch as if to knit. Insert left-hand needle into front of these 2 stitches and knit them together through the back loops

K2tog—Knit two stitches together as one stitch

YO—Yarn over

Dbl dec -Slip first and second stitches together as if to knit. Knit 1 stitch. Pass two slipped stitches over the knit stitch.

CN Cable Needle/Hook

C3 over 3 left -sl3 to CN, hold in front. k3, k3 from CN

Cast off—Bind off Stitch

M—(m1) cast on stitch The cast on stitch is used to add the additional leaves on either side of the center leaf.

Materials Needed:

Size 6(4.0 mm) straight knitting needles

2 balls of Lion Brand Cotton Ease 50% cotton 50% acrylic 207 yards. Apprx 300 yards needed.

Darning Needle

Cable Hook/needle

Pattern Notes:

Oats is a quick moving scarf that can be knit in any type of yarn. Large leaves are created with a series of increases and decreases while a simple cable is used in the center.

Any yarn weight or type may be used for this scarf. If using a different weight, take the suggested needle size and go up approx 2 sizes and test a small sample. This will help determine the appropriate needle for the alternative yarn.

Oats Scarf

Page 12

Co **12 stitches** on size 6 (4.0mm) straight knitting needles using long tail cast on method

Work 1 row k3, p6, k3 as a setup row and then begin working lace pattern from row 1. **All even rows are worked as they are seen with the yarn overs purled. You may wish to slip the first stitch of each row in order to create a border stitch.**

Please note: to create the additional Oats on either side 9 stitches must be cast on. Cast on 9 stitches on the wrong side row 20 and at the end of the right side row 21.

R1 (RS): p3, k6, p3 (12 stitches)

R3: p3, c3 over 3 left, p3 (12 stitches)

R5: p3, k6, p3 (12 stitches)

R7: p3, k3, yo, m1, yo, k3, p3 (15 stitches)

R9: p3, k3, yo, k3, yo, k3, p3 (17 stitches)

R11: p3, k3, yo, k5, yo, k3, p3 (19 stitches)

R13: p3, k3, yo, k2, k2tog, yo, k3, yo, k3, p3 (21 stitches)

R15: p3, k3, yo, k2, k2tog, yo, k1, yo, ssk, k2, yo, k3, p3 (23 stitches)

R17: p3, k3, yo, k2tog 2 times, yo, k3, yo, ssk 2 times, yo, k3, p3 (23 stitches)

R19: p3, k3, yo, k2tog, k2, yo, dbl dec, yo, k2, ssk, yo, k3, p3 (23 stitches)

R20: work entire row as knit the knits and purl the purls , purling the yarn overs, then cast on 9 stitches (32 stitches)

R21: p3, k6, p3, k3, yo, k2tog 2 times, yo, k3, yo, ssk 2 times, yo, k3, p3, m1 9 times (41 stitches)

R23: p3, k6, p3, k3, yo, k2tog, k2, yo, dbl dec, yo, k2, ssk, yo, k3, p3, k6, p3 (41 stitches)

R25: p3, c3 over 3 left, p3, k3, yo, k2tog 2 times, yo, k3, yo, ssk 2 times, yo, k3, p3, c3 over 3 left, p3 (41 stitches)

R27: p3, k6, p3, k2, ssk, yo, k2tog, k1, yo, dbl dec, yo, k1, ssk, yo, k2tog, k2, p3, k6, p3 (39 stitches)

R29: p3, k3, yo, m1, yo, k3, p3, k2, ssk, yo, k2tog, k3, ssk, yo, k2tog, k2, p3, k3, yo, m1, yo, k3, p3 (43 stitches)

R31: p3, k3, yo, k3, yo, k3, p3, k2, ssk, yo, k2tog, k1, ssk, yo, k2tog, k2, p3, k3, yo, k3, yo, k3, p3 (45 stitches)

R33: p3, k3, yo, k5, yo, k3, p3, k2, ssk, yo, dbl dec, yo, k2tog, k2, p3, k3, yo, k5, yo, k3, p3 (47 stitches)

R35: p3, k3, yo, k2, k2tog, yo, k3, yo, k3, p3, k3, dbl dec, k3, p3, k3, yo, k2, k2tog, yo, k3, yo, k3, p3 (49 stitches)

R37: p3, k3, yo, k2, k2tog, yo, k1, yo, ssk, k2, yo, k3, p3, k2, ssk, k3, p3, k3, yo, k2, k2tog, yo, k1, yo, ssk, k2, yo, k3, p3 (52 stitches)

R39: p3, k3, yo, k2tog 2 times, yo, k3, yo, ssk 2 times, yo, k3, p3, c3 over 3 left, p3, k3, yo, k2tog 2 times, yo, k3, yo, ssk 2 times, yo, k3, p3

(52 stitches)

R41: p3, k3, yo, k2tog, k2, yo, dbl dec, yo, k2, ssk, yo, k3, p3, k6, p3, k3, yo, k2tog, k2, yo, dbl dec, yo, k2, ssk, yo, k3, p3 (52 stitches)

R43: p3, k3, yo, k2tog 2 times, yo, k3, yo, ssk 2 times, yo, k3, p3, k6, p3, k3, yo, k2tog 2 times, yo, k3, yo, ssk 2 times, yo, k3, p3

(52 stitches)

R45: p3, k3, yo, k2tog, k2, yo, dbl dec, yo, k2, ssk, yo, k3, p3, c3 over 3 left, p3, k3, yo, k2tog, k2, yo, dbl dec, yo, k2, ssk, yo, k3, p3

(52 stitches)

R47: p3, k3, yo, k2tog 2 times, yo, k3, yo, ssk 2 times, yo, k3, p3, k6, p3, k3, yo, k2tog 2 times, yo, k3, yo, ssk 2 times, yo, k3, p3

(52 stitches)

R49: p3, k2, ssk, yo, k2tog, k1, yo, dbl dec, yo, k1, ssk, yo, k2tog, k2, p3, k6, p3, k2, ssk, yo, k2tog, k1, yo, dbl dec, yo, k1, ssk, yo, k2tog, k2, p3 (48 stitches)

R51: p3, k2, ssk, yo, k2tog, k3, ssk, yo, k2tog, k2, p3, c3 over 3 left, p3, k2, ssk, yo, k2tog, k3, ssk, yo, k2tog, k2, p3 (44 stitches)

R53: p3, k2, ssk, yo, k2tog, k1, ssk, yo, k2tog, k2, p3, k6, p3, k2, ssk, yo, k2tog, k1, ssk, yo, k2tog, k2, p3 (40 stitches)

Oats Scarf

Page 13

R55: p3, k2, ssk, yo, dbl dec, yo, k2tog, k2, p3, k6, p3, k2, ssk, yo, dbl dec, yo, k2tog, k2, p3 (36 stitches)

R57: p3, k3, dbl dec, k3, p3, c3 over 3 left, p3, k3, dbl dec, k3, p3 (32 stitches)

R59: p3, k2, ssk, k3, p3, k6, p3, k2, ssk, k3, p3 (30 stitches)

R61: p3, k6, p3, k6, p3, k6, p3 (30 stitches)

R63: p3, c3 over 3 left, p3, c3 over 3 left, p3, c3 over 3 left, p3 (30 stitches)

R65: p3, k6, p3, k6, p3, k6, p3 (30 stitches)

Row 67—108 is repeated 3 or more times until you reach desired length. Sample scarf is repeated 3 times then Finish through Row 108, then complete Chart 3/Rows 109-175

R67: p3, k6, p3, k6, p3, k6, p3 (30 stitches)

R69: p3, c3 over 3 left, p3, c3 over 3 left, p3, c3 over 3 left, p3 (30 stitches)

R71: p3, k6, p3, k6, p3, k6, p3 (30 stitches)

R73: p3, k3, yo, m1, yo, k3, p3, k6, p3, k3, yo, m1, yo, k3, p3 (36 stitches)

R75: p3, k3, yo, k3, yo, k3, p3, c3 over 3 left, p3, k3, yo, k3, yo, k3, p3 (40 stitches)

R77: p3, k3, yo, k5, yo, k3, p3, k6, p3, k3, yo, k5, yo, k3, p3 (44 stitches)

R79: p3, k3, yo, k2, k2tog, yo, k3, yo, k3, p3, k6, p3, k3, yo, k2, k2tog, yo, k3, yo, k3, p3 (48 stitches)

R81: p3, k3, yo, k2, k2tog, yo, k1, yo, ssk, k2, yo, k3, p3, c3 over 3 left, p3, k3, yo, k2, k2tog, yo, k1, yo, ssk, k2, yo, k3, p3 (52 stitches)

R83: p3, k3, yo, k2tog 2 times, yo, k3, yo, ssk 2 times, yo, k3, p3, k6, p3, k3, yo, k2tog 2 times, yo, k3, yo, ssk 2 times, yo, k3, p3 (52 stitches)

R85: p3, k3, yo, k2tog, k2, yo, dbl dec, yo, k2, ssk, yo, k3, p3, k6, p3, k3, yo, k2tog, k2, yo, dbl dec, yo, k2, ssk, yo, k3, p3 (52 stitches)

R87: p3, k3, yo, k2tog 2 times, yo, k3, yo, ssk 2 times, yo, k3, p3, c3 over 3 left, p3, k3, yo, k2tog 2 times, yo, k3, yo, ssk 2 times, yo, k3, p3 (52 stitches)

R89: p3, k3, yo, k2tog, k2, yo, dbl dec, yo, k2, ssk, yo, k3, p3, k6, p3, k3, yo, k2tog, k2, yo, dbl dec, yo, k2, ssk, yo, k3, p3 (52 stitches)

R91: p3, k3, yo, k2tog 2 times, yo, k3, yo, ssk 2 times, yo, k3, p3, k6, p3, k3, yo, k2tog 2 times, yo, k3, yo, ssk 2 times, yo, k3, p3 (52 stitches)

R93: p3, k2, ssk, yo, k2tog, k1, yo, dbl dec, yo, k1, ssk, yo, k2tog, k2, p3, c3 over 3 left, p3, k2, ssk, yo, k2tog, k1, yo, dbl dec, yo, k1, ssk, yo, k2tog, k2, p3 (48 stitches)

R95: p3, k2, ssk, yo, k2tog, k3, ssk, yo, k2tog, k2, p3, k6, p3, k2, ssk, yo, k2tog, k3, ssk, yo, k2tog, k2, p3 (44 stitches)

R97: p3, k2, ssk, yo, k2tog, k1, ssk, yo, k2tog, k2, p3, k6, p3, k2, ssk, yo, k2tog, k1, ssk, yo, k2tog, k2, p3 (40 stitches)

R99: p3, k2, ssk, yo, dbl dec, yo, k2tog, k2, p3, c3 over 3 left, p3, k2, ssk, yo, dbl dec, yo, k2tog, k2, p3 (36 stitches)

R101: p3, k3, dbl dec, k3, p3, k6, p3, k3, dbl dec, k3, p3 (32 stitches)

R103: p3, k2, ssk, k3, p3, k6, p3, k2, ssk, k3, p3 (30 stitches)

R105: p3, c3 over 3 left, p3, c3 over 3 left, p3, c3 over 3 left, p3 (30 stitches)

R107: p3, k6, p3, k6, p3, k6, p3 (30 stitches)

Repeat the above pattern until garment reaches desired length Then begin working chart 3. for the charted and pattern 3 for the written.

Pattern 3—this section is used once you have reached the desired length and you are ready to finish the opposite end of the scarf.

R109: p3, k6, p3, k6, p3, k6, p3 (30 stitches)

R111: p3, c3 over 3 left, p3, c3 over 3 left, p3, c3 over 3 left, p3 (30 stitches)

R113: p3, k6, p3, k6, p3, k6, p3 (30 stitches)

R115: p3, k3, yo, m1, yo, k3, p3, k6, p3, k3, yo, m1, yo, k3, p3 (36 stitches)

Oats Scarf

Page 14

R117: p3, k3, yo, k3, yo, k3, p3, c3 over 3 left, p3, k3, yo, k3, yo, k3, p3 (40 stitches)

R119: p3, k3, yo, k5, yo, k3, p3, k6, p3, k3, yo, k5, yo, k3, p3 (44 stitches)

R121: p3, k3, yo, k2, k2tog, yo, k3, yo, k3, p3, k6, p3, k3, yo, k2, k2tog, yo, k3, yo, k3, p3 (48 stitches)

R123: p3, k3, yo, k2, k2tog, yo, k1, yo, ssk, k2, yo, k3, p3, c3 over 3 left, p3, k3, yo, k2, k2tog, yo, k1, yo, ssk, k2, yo, k3, p3 (52 stitches)

R125: p3, k3, yo, k2tog 2 times, yo, k3, yo, ssk 2 times, yo, k3, p3, k6, p3, k3, yo, k2tog 2 times, yo, k3, yo, ssk 2 times, yo, k3, p3 (52 stitches)

R127: p3, k3, yo, k2tog, k2, yo, dbl dec, yo, k2, ssk, yo, k3, p3, k6, p3, k3, yo, k2tog, k2, yo, dbl dec, yo, k2, ssk, yo, k3, p3 (52 stitches)

R129: p3, k3, yo, k2tog 2 times, yo, k3, yo, ssk 2 times, yo, k3, p3, c3 over 3 left, p3, k3, yo, k2tog 2 times, yo, k3, yo, ssk 2 times, yo, k3, p3 (52 stitches)

R131: p3, k3, yo, k2tog, k2, yo, dbl dec, yo, k2, ssk, yo, k3, p3, k6, p3, k3, yo, k2tog, k2, yo, dbl dec, yo, k2, ssk, yo, k3, p3 (52 stitches)

R133: p3, k3, yo, k2tog 2 times, yo, k3, yo, ssk 2 times, yo, k3, p3, k3, yo, m1, yo, k3, p3, k3, yo, k2tog 2 times, yo, k3, yo, ssk 2 times, yo, k3, p3 (55 stitches)

R135: p3, k2, ssk, yo, k2tog, k1, yo, dbl dec, yo, k1, ssk, yo, k2tog, k2, p3, k3, yo, k3, yo, k3, p3, k2, ssk, yo, k2tog, k1, yo, dbl dec, yo, k1, ssk, yo, k2tog, k2, p3 (53 stitches)

R137: p3, k2, ssk, yo, k2tog, k3, ssk, yo, k2tog, k2, p3, k3, yo, k5, yo, k3, p3, k2, ssk, yo, k2tog, k3, ssk, yo, k2tog, k2, p3 (51 stitches)

R139: p3, k2, ssk, yo, k2tog, k1, ssk, yo, k2tog, k2, p3, k3, yo, k2, k2tog, yo, k3, yo, k3, p3, k2, ssk, yo, k2tog, k1, ssk, yo, k2tog, k2, p3 (49 stitches)

R141: p3, k2, ssk, yo, dbl dec, yo, k2tog, k2, p3, k3, yo, k2, k2tog, yo, k1, yo, ssk, k2, yo, k3, p3, k2, ssk, yo, dbl dec, yo, k2tog, k2, p3 (47 stitches)

R143: p3, k3, dbl dec, k3, p3, k3, yo, k2tog 2 times, yo, k3, yo, ssk 2 times, yo, k3, p3, k3, dbl dec, k3, p3 (43 stitches)

R145: p3, k2, ssk, k3, p3, k3, yo, k2tog, k2, yo, dbl dec, yo, k2, ssk, yo, k3, p3, k2, ssk, k3, p3 (41 stitches)

R147: p3, c3 over 3 left, p3, k3, yo, k2tog 2 times, yo, k3, yo, ssk 2 times, yo, k3, p3, c3 over 3 left, p3 (41 stitches)

R149: p3, k6, p3, k3, yo, k2tog, k2, yo, dbl dec, yo, k2, ssk, yo, k3, p3, k6, p3 (41 stitches)

R151: COS 9 times, p3, k3, yo, k2tog 2 times, yo, k3, yo, ssk 2 times, yo, k3, p3, k6, p3, k3 (32 stitches)

R152: COS 9 times then complete the row knitting the knits and purling the purls. (23 stitches)

R153: p3, k2, ssk, yo, k2tog, k1, yo, dbl dec, yo, k1, ssk, yo, k2tog, k2, p3 (21 stitches)

R155: p3, k2, ssk, yo, k2tog, k3, ssk, yo, k2tog, k2, p3 (19 stitches)

R157: p3, k2, ssk, yo, k2tog, k1, ssk, yo, k2tog, k2, p3 (17 stitches)

R159: p3, k2, ssk, yo, dbl dec, yo, k2tog, k2, p3 (15 stitches)

R161: p3, k3, dbl dec, k3, p3 (13 stitches)

R163: p3, k2, ssk, k3, p3 (12 stitches)

R165: p3, k6, p3 (12 stitches)

R167: p3, c3 over 3 left, p3 (12 stitches)

R169: p3, k6, p3 (12 stitches)

R171: COS 12 times

Oats Scarf

Page 15

Chart Abbreviations

Please note—the M—make one should be worked as a cast on stitch .
See written instructions for more information.

No Stitch
Placeholder - No stitch made.

purl
purl stitch

knit
knit stitch

c3 over 3 left
sl3 to CN, hold in front. k3, k3 from CN

yo
Yarn Over

make one
Cast on stitch for additional leaf

k2tog
Knit two stitches together as one stitch

ssk
Slip one stitch as if to knit, Slip another stitch as if to knit. Insert left-hand needle into front of these 2 stitches and knit them together

Cast On
Cast on stitch

Central Double Dec
Slip first and second stitches together as if to knit. Knit 1 stitch. Pass two slipped stitches over the knit stitch.

Cast Off Stitch
Bind off Stitch

Oats Scarf

Chart 1 Rows 1—65

Chart is worked from right to left with all wrong sides worked as seen, purling the yarn overs.

The cast on is on row 20 at the end of the wrong side row.

Oats Scarf

Chart 2 Rows 67—107 which is the repeat not showing wrong side row of 108

Page 17

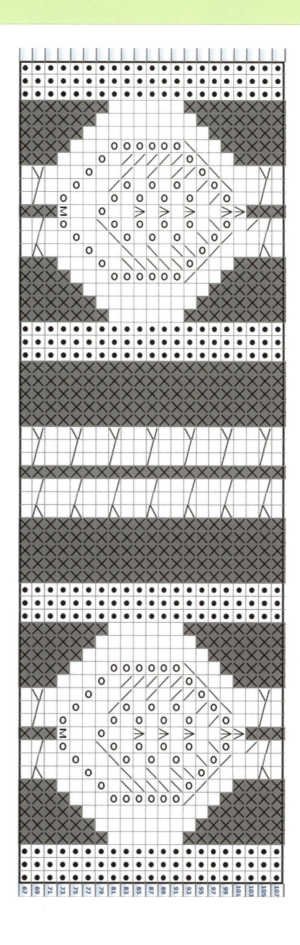

Oats Scarf

Chart 3 Rows 109 to 171

On row 151 the bind off in the black boxes will be bound off on row 152

Page 18

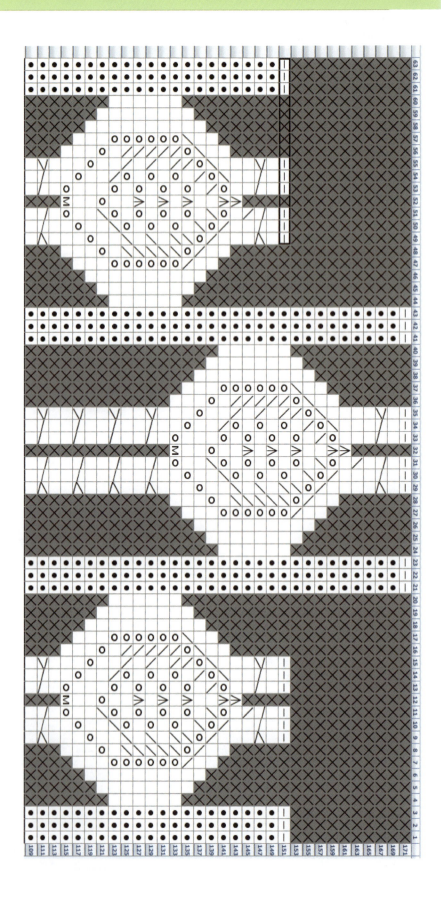

Printed in Great Britain
by Amazon.co.uk, Ltd.,
Marston Gate.